PRAISE FOR A PL

MW00772390

"More and more, pre-teens and teenagers are going through life battling issues they sometimes believe no one can truly understand. Thankfully, there is now a book written not just for preteens and teenagers, but for people from all walks of life, regardless of their age, gender, religion, or race.

"This book brings to life the many hidden issues pre-teens and teenagers struggle with every day. In reading this book you will find out how one young girl was able to ride the waves and weather the storms of her teenage years with prayer, family, and friends.

"Her story, told from the heart, takes you into the depth of her struggles with cutting, anxiety, depression, anorexia, and suicide. Shannon bared it all and, through her story, hopes to help other young girls and boys overcome these struggles. The details are visual, and with the turn of each page you are left wanting to read more on how she broke the chains and became free."

SHERIKA DACRES
MIDDLE SCHOOL TEACHER

"This extraordinary young woman has generously shared her personal struggle through pain, despair, and self-destructive experiences in adolescence to the other side of enthusiastically embracing life in young adulthood. To read this book is to travel with her and to believe there is hope for others. I look forward to a sequel."

MARGARET A. FOLEY
LCSW SOCIAL WORKER

"Shannon Rowell's personal experiences and difficult journey at a young age continue to help many young teens and their parents navigate through tumultuous times. As a busy, working mother, Shannon provided me with incredible insight into the thoughts and feelings of my own children. I'm incredibly grateful for the guidance she gave me."

KATHY SWANSON
FORMER PRESIDENT WINNIE PALMER HOSPITAL

"Written by a brave young woman who took her frightening teenage experiences and shared with others, so young people and parents like myself could learn and really believe that there is light, happiness, fulfillment, and real joy at the end of a very dark tunnel."

SUZANNE ALLEN
MOTHER OF A RECOVERED CHILD

"The insight that Shannon gives in her book is invaluable. We all hope and pray that our children, siblings, or friends will never go through these hard times that can bring on an unhealthy behavior or habits, but to be honest it happens more often than you would think. It has personally happened to some of the people closest to me that I thought were the most confident and unshakable people I knew. It can sneak up and bite you. Knowing what signs to look out for and how to reach out or encourage those we love is so very delicate and important. Shannon, through her own life experiences and also her counseling expertise, gives you the tools you need and a sneak peek into the mind of those suffering. Reading this book can equip you for these heartbreaking realities that so many of our loved one's face in their daily lives."

"Compelling and insightful. Shannon Rowell takes you on a journey from pain and suffering to healing and recovery. This book is a message of hope in the midst of darkness; written with honesty and transparency… a must read."

"A must read for anyone struggling with self-destructive tendencies during their formative years. Having known Shannon personally during the end of the most caustic chapter of her adolescent years, seeing her thrive in her adult life is to see the living manifestation of hope, perseverance, and happiness."

A
Purpose
for the Pain

Shannon Leigh Rowell

Shannon Leigh Rowell

A Purpose

for the
Pain

*Finding freedom
from self-harm, anxiety,
depression, anorexia,
and suicide*

A Purpose for the Pain: Finding freedom from self-harm, anxiety, depression, anorexia, and suicide

by Shannon Leigh Rowell

Published by HigherLife Development Services, Inc.
PO Box 623307
Oviedo, Florida 32765
407.463.4806
www.ahigherlife.com

Disclaimer: While each of the stories shared is based on truthful circumstances, they have been updated to protect all parties involved.

Cover Design: William Diggs

10 11 12 13—9 8 7 6 5 4 3 2 1

Printed in the United States of America

DEDICATION

To my mom and dad: I dedicate this book to my wonderful parents, Marshall and Sherrie Sitarik. I thank both of you for your continued support and encouragement in my life. You have both believed in me when very few people were willing. Although I have put you through more than any parent should have to experience with their child, I thank you from the bottom of my heart for choosing to never give up on me. I have learned a tremendous amount from my experiences and hope to make you proud by using my story to help others. Thank you for guiding me and staying with me each step of the way. I love you!

To my husband: I now understand if I hadn't taken the path God gave me, I would not have been led to the love of my life, Steven Rowell. You are truly an amazing blessing and a wonderful man. I thank you for your unconditional love and support. I couldn't have achieved my many dreams without your encouragement. You are my stronghold, and I thank God for you each and every day. Thank you for loving me the way you do. I love you!

Special Thanks: I would like to offer a special thank you to my sister, Stacey Lynn Gratzon (married name). I know it wasn't always easy for you to experience the trauma I experienced. I feel I have put you through a tremendous amount of stress at such a young age—but no matter the cost, you have always been by my side. I want to thank you for being such a wonderful sister and best friend.

I would also like to recognize my grandmother, Beatrix Sitarik. You have always held a special place in my heart. Thank you for being my anchor when I needed you the most. I couldn't have gotten through this hard time without your love and support.

TABLE OF CONTENTS

POEMS

All poems by Shannon Leigh Rowell

ILLUSTRATIONS

All illustrations by Shannon Leigh Rowell

PROLOGUE

I am sitting here staring out in the distance… There is a young girl. She looks as if she hasn't got a friend in the world to talk with. I can't help but wonder what she is thinking or why she looks so lonely. Surely, she is normal, just like anyone else her age. There is no way she could have ever experienced what I have been through. So why does she look so sad? Why does she frown when everyone around her smiles?

Then she looks in my direction. Our eyes lock, and it is then I realize the girl I am watching is…me.

Perhaps you feel as I did. One minute you are scared and insecure, and the next, secure. You laugh and cry with the greatest of force in your life. You feel alone, scared, and confused. Suddenly, change is the enemy, and you cling to the past with dear life. Soon you realize the past is wandering farther and farther away, and there is nothing to do but stay where you are or move forward. This is when you are faced with making your next life decision.

Which will you choose?

Commit to the Lord
whatever you do and your
plans will succeed.

Proverbs 16:3

INTRODUCTION

This book is not for the faint of heart. I have pondered quite often if I would even want to write out my story for others to read. I realized not everyone wants to have a conversation about their personal life experiences or let a complete stranger know their deep inner thoughts and feelings. I do know, however, that many young people are going through experiences very similar to what I have been through. I am sure some of these individuals are afraid, for whatever reason, to tell someone or ask for help. As much as I would like my story to help everyone, I know this is unrealistic. I want this book to help not only teens and young adults who have a similar background to mine, but also to help parents understand what their child or someone close to them may be experiencing.

If you start to read this and are unable to relate or are just not interested, then this book may not be meant for you. However, if you start to read and find yourself longing for more understanding, then I encourage you to keep reading. My goal is to share with you a story many people would deem too personal to share with others. I am opening my heart to you now because I know without a doubt that everything happens for a reason, and there is always hope in this forever chaotic world.

CHAPTER ONE

A Young Girl Searching

If you looked at my life from the outside, you would see what appeared to be an almost perfectly normal life. I have a mother and father who have never been divorced, a younger sister, and have always had a family dog growing up. My grandma has always had a great presence in my life and even lived with my family as I grew up. I have attended the most prestigious private Christian schools and have always lived what I would call a comfortable life.

My parents would tell you I was the perfect little girl. I used to ask permission just to get out of bed in the morning. However, once I started to hit my teenage years, my life took a major turn. In fact, even now it is hard for me to remember some of what I experienced. To help me cope I have blocked a lot of hurtful and awful memories, but there are still some I just can't erase no matter how hard I try.

The majority of my problems began when I was thirteen years old. I attended a very small, private Christian middle school in Orlando, Florida. My parents wanted me to attend a Christian school to help reinforce the beliefs of our family.

At that time, we attended church and would go to service every Sunday morning.

As I got older, I decided I wanted to attend a youth group at another church where some of my friends attended. My parents were reluctant but eventually agreed. On Wednesday nights, they would drop me off for youth group where I would meet some of my friends. During the second week of youth group, I met a boy named Timothy who was a little older than me.

I was immediately attracted to the vibe he gave off. He dressed and talked differently than the people I usually hung out with. He wore black baggy pants, usually with a black Korn shirt (Korn was a popular rock band at the time). He was more confident than other guys I had met and had a punk style about him. His hair was a very dark chocolate color, almost black, and curly. We became friends almost immediately.

Eventually, instead of attending youth group on Wednesday nights, a group of us would meet and walk to the nearby McDonald's to hang out until the time youth group ended. After several weeks, Timothy introduced our group to another so-called religion, Wicca. I was enthralled by the darkness of this Wicca experience and tried to learn as much as I could under Timothy's guidance. He gave me a couple of books to take home to study and said when I saw him the next week, he would explain anything I didn't understand.

Back at school, I introduced my two closest friends to Wicca, and in after-school care we would practice the different rituals we read about. Since the school was so small, we would usually block off the girls' bathroom, turn off the lights, and dive into the different rituals explained in the book.

At first it all seemed harmless and fun. The girls' bathroom had a long countertop, and one of us would usually lay on the counter while the other two girls summoned spirits around her. I think we would even spook ourselves and just think things were happening around us that really weren't.

The Wiccan rituals were, however, a form of witchcraft. I soon became so involved in them that I would study and practice under my parents' roof, and I knew I had gotten into the heavier stuff when the nightmares started.

Almost every night I had a recurring nightmare of four dark hooded figures appearing out of my closets. They would stand over me as I was sleeping and whisper to me. They would tell me to kill myself or hurt others to help release the pain I was feeling. Each night the nightmares went further and became more vivid. Although I was sleeping, it felt so real.

I could feel the cold energy as they placed their hands slightly above my body. I could hear the whispers as they spoke to me, getting louder each time they appeared. There were nights when I would try to tell myself to wake up, but I just couldn't. When I did finally wake up, I was drenched in sweat and often wondered if it truly was just a dream.

Whispers

November 15, 1999

Voices in my head tell me,
They whisper evil thoughts
To make me believe.
They say it won't hurt.
It will happen so fast;
That I won't feel a thing,
And the day will finally be my last.
I guess I'm starting to believe
There's tons of ways to do it,
As long as I make myself bleed.
I'm really starting to think,
Should I use this knife?
Take these pills lying here?
Or just find another way to take my
    life?
You ask why should I do it.
Well, if you knew what I've been going
    through you'd probably be
    debating it too. Okay, I'm standing
    on the edge.
I take the knife; stab it in my chest,
and finally fall off the ledge.
That's it, I did it!
The voices are gone,
My family's upset,
And now I don't have to go on.

4

With each passing day I fell deeper into a depressed state. I felt like I was literally falling in a dark hole with no way out. It was a horrible feeling because I didn't know or even understand why I felt so empty inside. I quickly became anorexic and slept all the time.

When I was awake, I was so miserable others didn't want to be around me. I started to think of ways to make the inner pain stop, and then I remembered what the hooded figures in my nightmares told me. I started to think of ways to kill myself, but I wasn't even sure it was something I could really do.

For the next couple of months, I wrote a lot. I started writing poetry to get what I was feeling out and onto paper, but it wasn't enough. Every moment I had, I would sleep or write. As long as I slept, I didn't feel the pain. I didn't have to constantly feel like a knife was penetrating my heart, and I didn't have to be around anyone. I just couldn't take it anymore. I didn't even know why I felt so much pain in my life.

One night I was lying with my mom in her bedroom, as I usually did to spend time with her, and I mustered up the courage to tell her I didn't want to live anymore. As you can imagine, this took her by surprise. She immediately asked me questions and soon realized I was experiencing something very deep and painful that would require professional help.

Suicidal Note

May 17, 1999

I say good-bye to my friends and
family and to all the people who have
hurt me. I say good-bye to my dog
So that I might go to heaven and be
    with God.
I'm sorry I have to tell you this way,
But there's really not much more I can
    say.
I'm tired of my life so I have to go,
But remember, Mom, how much I love
    you so.
I can't live in misery anymore,
for my heart's already been torn.
And I want you to remember it's not
    your fault.
I chose to do this
To get away from it all.
Remember I love you
But now I must say good-bye.
You are the best parents
So please don't cry.

Please note that I did not intend to give this note to my parents. Writing poetry was an outlet for me, and although I was contemplating suicide, I chose to express my feelings on paper rather than through actions.

Things I wish I had known:

- Feelings of loneliness along with hormonal changes are normal in the teenage years. The adolescence phase is a time of personal and emotional growth. It is the time where adolescents are developing their own identities. It is also the time where outside influence has its greatest impact.

- During this time the brain is still developing and, because of this, adolescents face certain emotional barriers. The prefrontal cortex is the last part of the brain to reach maturation, which isn't realized until 25-30 years of age. The prefrontal cortex is often referred to as the "CEO" of the brain because it is responsible for executive functioning. The executive functions include organizing thoughts, focusing attention, problem solving, being able to see possible future problems and weighing the consequences, controlling impulses, and controlling emotions.

- Because adolescents lack the above functions, it is no wonder why they think and behave the way they do. It's a confusing time.

- Asking someone for help is okay and nothing to be afraid of. Most people are very understanding and are happy to get you the help you need.

- During adolescence, it can be scary to ask others for help. Many teens fear they will get into trouble or will be seen as crazy. They wonder what will happen when someone finds out what they are going through. All these fears are normal and valid.

- Sometimes it can be hard to know where to go to ask for help. Personally, I would suggest going to the person you are emotionally closest with. This can be a youth pastor, teacher, guidance counselor, relative, neighbor, parent, or sibling. An adult would be the best option, as they are best equipped and will know what resources are best for your situation.

- Choosing to explore the religion of Christianity in other denominations would have helped develop my own spiritual identity.

- It is normal for adolescents to go through a period where they start to question a lot of their upbringing. Sometimes this will include questioning the very religion their parents raised them in. Most of the time teenagers will return to the foundation that was laid out for them throughout childhood, but it's important to note that questioning religions or different denominations of a certain religion may not always be about the actual spiritual identity. Teenagers love to test boundaries.

As a parent now:

- When you see a behavior or mood change in your teenager, it means you should investigate further. There is, most likely, something going on in your teens life that is confusing and overwhelming. Not all teenagers will choose to be open with their parents, but if parents can communicate that they will listen without judgement, then teenagers will be more likely to come to them during times of need.

- Lay the foundation for your family's faith but never force your teenager into believing. They will need to explore for themselves so their faith decision becomes their own. From a young age, it is important to prepare your child for things that might happen in the future. For instance, around the pre-teen years (or even before), parents can tell their children it is normal to start questioning their faith as they become older and more independent. This allows for a teenager to then remember what their parents said when and if they ever do begin to question their religion/beliefs.

- Never stop communicating with your teen. Teenagers like to feel they have control over their lives. Talking down or at them will only make them shut down more. It is important to validate their feelings and ideas so they feel they are being heard, and they will be more willing to talk openly.

CHAPTER TWO

Funny Farm

The day after I told my mom my thoughts, I went to school like normal—except the day turned out to be far from any other normal day. Then again, I don't think I even knew what normal was anymore. Right after class was dismissed for lunch, I saw my mom and her best friend coming down the hallway.

I was surprised to see them, and when I approached them, my mom was barely able to speak to me because she was sad and upset. Her best friend took me in her arms and told me that I needed to come with them. I soon learned I would be going to a psychiatric treatment facility because I was having "suicidal ideations," which is just fancy talk for having thoughts about killing myself.

I cried all the way home. I was told to go to my room and pack a couple of different outfits because they didn't know how long I would be in the hospital. As soon as I got to my room, I quickly picked up the phone and dialed my then-boyfriend Nick and told him what was going on. I can't remember the extent of our conversation, but I remember him being supportive and trying to calm me down.

Imagine being a thirteen-year-old girl and being told you are going to be hospitalized for having thoughts of hurting yourself. I was terrified! Why were my parents doing this to me, and what would they decide to do if they knew even half of what I was into? So, I kept the nightmares and Wicca a secret just a little bit longer.

When we got to the hospital, my mom and her friend registered me. I was so mad at my mom that I didn't even say goodbye. My heart was pounding and tears flowed down my cheeks. I was hot, literally. My hands were sweating, and I felt like I couldn't breathe. I wasn't crazy! I didn't belong in a place like this. What if the others in the center hurt me? There were so many thoughts and feelings going through my head.

I gave my mom's friend a hug and walked down a long hallway with a nurse. My mother worked at the same organization as this hospital, so they told me I should register under an alias. I was furious and felt like my mom didn't want to be associated with me. I felt she was ashamed of me for being in the hospital.

I chose my best friend's last name and was given an armband. The only perk to my mother's position was getting my own room. Usually, patients have to share a room that has a pair of twin beds, a dresser, and one bathroom. The walls were bright white and the floor was utterly cold. I can remember the empty feeling of sitting in my room. It was very depressing.

As I entered my room, the nurse told me she would need to do a skin check on me. *What the hell is that?* I wondered. *You want to do what? Are you crazy?* She told me to undress so that I could show her any marks on me. I was humiliated!

It was so cold, and I cried the entire time. I felt I was being stripped of my dignity.

If you are a parent reading this, you can probably empathize with my mom when she had to make this difficult decision to admit me to the psychiatric hospital. As angry as I was with her, I know she made this decision based on what she thought was best for me at the time. Just as any mother would do, this was the only way she felt I would be protected. I had to get out of my toxic environment and needed intense treatment.

Basket Case

It took a couple days before the doctor would even see me. Each day was the same, almost like the movie *Groundhog Day*—except I was in a more confined area. A typical day for me in the psychiatric center consisted of waking up early, having my vital signs taken, eating breakfast, cleaning my room, watching the morning news, group therapy, school, and some free time. Because I was anorexic, I was watched closely when it came to mealtime.

I remember trying to hide my food or give it away when no one was looking. *Why should they be able to choose whether I ate or not?* When it came time to have my vitals taken and be weighed, the staff made me turn backward on the scale so I couldn't see my weight. Every time I stepped foot on the scale, I felt I was growing bigger and bigger, and it only made me want to eat less to stop the thoughts of feeling fat.

Feeling Good

September 29, 1999

My body is feeling tired and alone
But yet I strive to be the smallest,
The only kind of my own.
When I look in the mirror all I see is fat.
People say I'm nothing but skin and bones
but it feels like I'm much more than that.
I starve myself thinking I'll be OK,
But when I listen to others,
"You're going to die" is all they say.
I want to feel good about myself
And if that means not eating
Then I'll do that and risk my health.
Sooner or later, I know I'll die,
But at least I felt good about myself
When I was still alive.

Free time consisted of watching television, reading, or developing my poetic skills. We would have to earn points to use the telephone, and we were required to call our parents at least once. Somehow, I always got around calling my parents and would call my boyfriend instead. He seemed like the only person not against me at the time.

I was in the center for more than two weeks and even had to spend my fourteenth birthday there. Do you think I got a cake or even gifts? No! When it came time for visitation, I was always excited to see my grandma. I missed her more than anyone. She always wrote me letters, and after each visit I would read them. Looking back, I can see how I was breaking her heart. My parents and I started to drift farther apart, and I wasn't able to see my sister because minors weren't allowed to visit. As much as we didn't get along at the time, there was always a part of me that longed for her to be near.

After a couple of days, I started opening up to some of the staff and other patients. I started to learn the right comments I should give to make it seem as if I was getting better.

There was one tech I remember the most from my time there. He read the poems I wrote and encouraged me to keep expressing myself through writing. That made such an impact on me that I wrote a poem dedicated to him while I was in the center.

Closed Doors

March 25,1999

Sitting quiet and still
in the darkest room;
I'm tired of begging and being here
Behind closed doors.
Nothing ever seems to work.
I'm very uncomfortable
And just want to leave this earth.
I don't need help;
Just want to be left alone
so I can be by myself.

I met a girl while I was hospitalized who was a few years older than me. We became good friends during my stay. As we exchanged stories, she told me of another way I could release the pain I was feeling without anyone noticing. That is how I learned to cut myself.

She told me she would cut herself with a blade or knife. She said it helped her release her anger and pain. Of course, I was up for anything at that point. I wanted to die, so this couldn't hurt. The only problem was being stuck in the psychiatric hospital where there were no sharp objects.

One day I asked for a picture out of my wallet, and when the nurse handed it to me, I realized I had left a Coke bottle cap in the front fold. I took it out with the picture so the nurse wouldn't notice. I quickly went back to my room and started to act as if I were reading a magazine. I had learned the schedule of the timed checkups the techs had to perform, so I knew I had exactly fifteen minutes to try to cut myself until they would be back to check on me.

I bit the cap in half and put it to my arm. I pushed down as hard as I could and dragged it across my arm until I saw the blood. After the initial slit it became so easy to keep going.

I remember it feeling so good to see and feel the blood starting to drip down my arm. I was able to carve the word vampire on my left arm that day—except I spelled the word wrong: VAMPIER. To keep anyone from noticing, I wore long sleeves and baggy sweatshirts all the time. No one suspected a thing because it was always cold in the hospital, so my cutting went unnoticed for the rest of my stay.

That was the day I became addicted to cutting, which became a lifelong battle. It felt great to finally control when I felt pain and to have the scars as a constant reminder of the pain I had inside.

Looking back, I can't believe how young I was when I started to feel and act the way I did. It's hard to believe that anyone would take a blade or any sharp object to their flesh and enjoy it. But I felt relieved when I cut myself. I could feel the pressure and flesh splitting. The blood smelled of iron and was warm as it dripped down my arm. I would let the wounds almost heal and then pick the scabs off to make it bleed again. Sometimes I would cut to punish myself for thoughts or feelings I had.

After two weeks of trying to fool the staff into thinking I was getting better, I received word that the doctors finally felt I was on the road to recovery and was ready to go home. I remember being terrified after leaving the hospital because I was now on my own. I didn't feel safe anymore and I didn't want to tell anyone I was scared because I didn't want to show any signs of weakness.

My first night home I had my best friend spend the night with me. I decided to show her my arm and told her how I learned to cut myself. I asked her not to tell anyone and promised I was only cutting to release the pain and not an attempt to kill myself. While she promised she would keep it a secret, my mom later found out when she walked in on me taking a bath. She was shocked and ran out of the room sobbing (the bathroom and four closets were all located inside my bedroom). At that moment I started to feel bad, a feeling I rarely felt toward others at the time.

I got dressed and went to talk to my mom. I found her in our backyard sitting in a chair, crying. I went up to her and gave her a hug. I told her I was really in need of help because I didn't care if I died. I didn't see a point to my life. My mom held me and told me she would never give up on me. She slept with me for many nights and almost never left my side. Whenever she had the chance, she would rub vitamin E oil on my scars to help them fade.

Fallen Soul

June 2, 2000

I wonder if there's a hole in my soul.
My life doesn't feel complete
and I feel I've fallen
In a complete and utterly dark hole.
The pain cuts within.
The hole gets deeper,
the cutting begins.

I was put into counseling right away and was taken to see a psychiatrist who prescribed me antidepressants. I was put on the highest dose, which later took me a year to wean off when I was feeling better. I began counseling with a pastor at a local church. After just one session, this Christian counselor told my mom to give up on me and that there was nothing anyone could ever do to help me. In fact, he told my mother there is a very low recovery rate for kids involved with cults. I was a lost cause. My mom was devastated but refused to believe him. I never did go back to that counselor. In fact, his own son later experienced some of the same things I was battling. Sadly, this boy took his own life. I'm not sure if this counselor decided to follow the same advice he had given my mother, but the end result was horrible.

My mother wouldn't give up on me. Instead, I kept seeing my psychiatrist and later saw another counselor who I liked a lot. For a while I started to get better. I stopped practicing Wicca and started to feel less pain. My poetry turned from dark and depressing to writing more about love. I still felt depressed a lot, and it took me awhile to convince myself to get out of bed at times, but I did graduate from middle school and convinced my parents it was time for me to stop attending private Christian schools. So off I went to my first public high school.

Things I wish I had known:

- My parents weren't against me. They were at a loss and wanted to get me help as fast as possible. As a teenager, it is so easy to think adults don't know anything about the hardships teenagers can go through. Peers are the biggest influence during this time, so trusting an adult during a difficult time is not the typical first course of action. It is important to remind your teenager how much you love them (unconditionally) and that getting them the help they need is done out of love and not hate.

- I felt pushed aside when my mother had me use a different last name than ours. I should have spoken up and told her how I felt, even if it wouldn't have made a difference. Let's be honest, teenagers are not the best communicators. They like to be heard but do not always know the best way to get their message across. I have found that when children do not want to express their feelings in words, they may do better expressing them in written form. Parents can suggest a parent-child journal that can be written in and passed back and forth between parents and the child, writing a letter to the person they are upset with (even if that letter is never shared), will still allow the release of pent-up anger. Video messages can also be used as a diary for communication.

- I wish someone would have prepared me for leaving the psychiatric hospital and re-entering into society.

As a licensed mental health counselor, I see a lot of teenagers who need to be placed under a Baker Act (see page 86-87 for explanation) and placed into the care of professionals at a psychiatric facility. I always make it a point to go over the process of being in the facility and what it might be like when released from the facility. It is a hard transition from being behind locked doors and on a daily schedule, to being open and free to do as you like. I remember feeling safe in the psychiatric facility and suddenly unsafe when I was sent home. It would have been easier for my parents and I to transition from the facility to home-life had we been better informed and prepared as to what to expect.

- Self-harm (cutting, piercing) is becoming more common as an unhealthy coping skill. Most self-harm is not a suicide attempt, and placing an individual in a psychiatric hospital for this alone is one of the worst decisions anyone can make. It sends the signal that the individual is not safe and the method chosen to help calm them, although unhealthy, was a bad decision. Instead, it is best to validate the individual's feelings and focus on the emotion itself and not the act of self-harm. Most of the time, individuals who self-harm feel very little pain. This is because the act of cutting/piercing releases endorphins in the brain, which are our good feeling hormones, and in return provide pleasure for that individual. This is how self-harm can become an addiction.

As a parent now:

- Pastors are not licensed mental health professionals. *Please choose a licensed mental healthcare provider for your teen.* So many people use pastors as their first stop to getting counseling. Pastors are great to see when seeking religious advice, but they are not equipped to handle mental health concerns. A licensed mental health professional receives at least seven years of training, if not more. While a pastor's advice may seem harmless, it may not always be in the best interest of a person suffering from mental health issues. I have heard clients say they sought help from a pastor first because it was cheaper than therapy, which can be expensive. However, when cost is an issue, parents have options, like asking for sliding scale pricing, using insurance, using out of network benefits, seeing an intern, or seeking help from a church counseling center. Either way, choose someone in the field who is trained to handle mental health needs.

- Teens can be manipulative. Keep the relationship close by listening and not offering any kind of judgement. The second a teenager feels judged by someone they will shut down, and some will turn to some form of manipulation. Manipulation can be used to gain more feelings of love and acceptance, to get what they want when they want it and to cover themselves after doing something wrong. You can help reduce the manipulation by keeping a close relationship; one that offers the chance to be heard, loved, and accepted.

CHAPTER THREE

A Taste of the Real World

I entered a public high school in ninth grade and it wasn't long before I met a few different people. I immediately became friends with people who identified as Goths. I started to wear all black clothes, heavy black makeup, and even had my hair partially red at times. I started to identify with them because I finally felt I fit in somewhere.

I met a guy named Damien in one of my classes. Like many other guys I met, he was much older than me. Are you starting to see a recurring theme yet?

We began to date, and during this time, I was introduced to drugs. I started to smoke a lot of marijuana, which is more informally known as weed. In fact, I got high before I ever tried smoking a cigarette.

They Called Him a Freak

November 7, 1998

Dressed in black
from head to toe;
Walking the streets
but staying low.
Never a word did he speak,
but it was with his looks
That made the people freak.
From his dead black hair,
To the dark makeup that he wore
Is what made the people's hearts tear.
And never once did anyone come near
To lend him a simple hand;
But instead, they watched in fear.
Because of the carvings on his arms,
it gave him a look
without a charm.
He was just like any other guy
but now he was all alone
because no one gave it a try
To understand the question, why?
So, they called him a FREAK!

My first encounter with weed was a complete adrena-line rush. Damien and I were in the car with a couple of our friends from school driving down the back roads of our town. We pulled over on a dirt road and lit a joint. Next thing I knew, they "hot boxed" the car, which means they sealed all the windows and doors so that smoke filled the air in the car. I didn't feel anything until we finally opened the car door to let the smoke out. As I stepped out, I was so dizzy

I could barely stand. Yet it was a freeing feeling, and I had only inhaled the secondhand smoke. After that day I started to smoke whenever I could get my hands on it. When I was high, I would do things I never thought of doing before, and I liked the risk. I became more outspoken and adventurous. I thought I was invincible.

I was living life free and loved every minute of it—yet I became more and more depressed, suicidal, anorexic, and addicted to cutting. My thinking soon became so distorted that at times I would try any drug or do anything harmful to myself because I thought it would take me one step closer to dying. Sometimes I didn't even know what I was taking.

I remember taking a drug once, and within minutes I started to feel foggy, dizzy, and disoriented. I was watching TV and, instead of seeing people, I was seeing their skeletons. I started to freak out, but the fear soon faded and the whole experience became enjoyable. I also liked the feeling because I was able to tune my family out and not care about what they had to say or what they were feeling. In addition to cutting, I started to pierce different body parts on my own. I loved the feeling of a needle penetrating my skin. I would later have to take the piercings out due to infections.

During this period of my life, I developed many unhealthy relationships. One night I was hanging out with one of my friends at the golf course where he worked. I remember talking to him as he was cleaning up the store. It was late and we were the only ones around. I followed him out to the course to help him clean up the golf balls that were on the ground. Next thing I knew he had me pinned down on the ground and was taking off my pants. I can remember telling him "No!" several times, but he raped me. For some reason I wasn't strong enough, physically or mentally, to struggle.

2 Beer Queer

September 2, 2003

My mind goes blank
On the clearest of days;
My brain has been shot,
frozen over in a haze.
My speech is slurred
and my lips are numb;
The limbs of my body
to slush they have become.
My stomach turns
And I begin to feel faint;
My feet give underneath me
but never yet a complaint.
My vision is blurred;
I can no longer see;
Everything becomes cold
and I no longer believe.
I'm starting to feel good,
yet tired it seems;
I passed out on my bed
no longer to be seen.

I went home and acted like nothing ever happened. I started to think I brought it on myself and that maybe it wasn't really considered rape because I didn't fight enough to make him stop. I did not tell anyone for several years. In fact, I still hung out with this guy on several other occasions. It wasn't until much later that I realized what had really taken place that night. I had several counselors over the years and when each one suspected that I had been sexually abused, I would adamantly deny it. I didn't want to believe it happened, and I didn't want anyone to know. It wasn't until seven years later that I actually told my mom. And my suspicions were right about how she would react. She started to cry and was so upset that I felt horrible!

I was only fifteen years old, and I had just experienced what no one should ever have to experience. I thought he was one of my friends. Why would a friend do something like that to someone? Did I truly deserve it? I remember it being very dark outside. It happened behind a bush. I have been back to that golf course since then and the bush is no longer there.

Why did this make me second guess what happened? It felt so real. I was cold. I remember I could feel the prickles of the grass and it made me itch. I could feel the pressure of his hands holding me down with his weight. I gave up and stopped fighting.

The recurring nightmares that I had previously returned soon after that night. This time, however, I had not only thoughts of killing myself but also thoughts of hurting others in my family. One night I woke up from a nightmare and started to scream. When my mom came into my room, she said I looked straight at her and started to curse. I don't remember what I said, but unfortunately, I do remember yelling. Although I wanted to stop, for some reason I couldn't. A couple of minutes later I snapped out of it and seemed myself again.

Although we weren't sure what that night was about, my mom prayed over my room and my closets, because this was where I used to practice the witchcraft. In fact, in one of my walk-in closets (which was more like a storage room) the light would turn on frequently in the middle of the night by itself. Eventually my parents put a deadbolt lock on that door to make me feel safer.

The light continued to flick on randomly. The dreams and pain I experienced became so intense I would literally hug the floor of my bedroom every night and cry. I would cry and cry and constantly ask God why He was keeping me alive. I would beg and plead for Him to let it all end. When nothing would happen, I would get so angry that I would start to cut myself again until the blood ran down my arm.

Unborn

August 24, 2000

Lord, are You there?
I call Your name,
but do You care?
Do You know the struggles and trials
That are within me?
I've surely prayed,
But now all I
Do is pay.
Guide me, Jesus,
set me free!
Keep Your promise
so I'll believe.

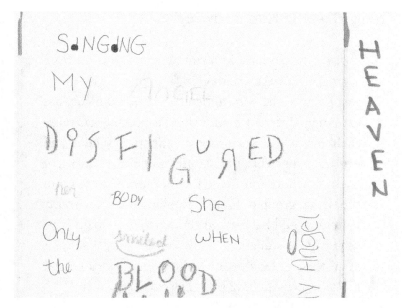

Disfigured Angel (2000)

My relationship with my father continued to grow even more distant. For some reason I would take everything out on him because I didn't trust him. I hated to be left alone in our house with him when my mom would have to work late nights. Although my dad never did anything inappropriate and would never intentionally hurt me, I was scared. I thought he might hurt me just as I was hurt on the golf course.

I felt I had no control over anything, except my weight— no control over my life or the direction it was heading. I didn't trust anyone anymore. When I would fall asleep at night, I would immediately wake up if anyone even came near my room. I could sense the slightest presence of anyone near me as I slept and would open my eyes to see who and why they were coming near me so late at night.

Things I wish I had known:

- I wish I would have known that the transition from a small Christian school to a public high school was going to be very difficult. Not just difficult but extremely different in almost all aspects. I was more sheltered while attending a Christian school and was not exposed to many different cultures, ideas, or clicks. I believe this made it easier for me to fall into the wrong group of friends. Looking back, I wish my parents would have asked the school if I could have shadowed a student. I know not all public schools allow this but looking into other options for an easier transition would have been helpful.

- I wish someone would have prepared me for the different "clicks" I would meet and to choose kids that would lift me up instead of bring me down. I am not sure I would have chosen differently, but because we didn't have different "clicks" in the Christian school I previously attended, I wasn't prepared. I chose to hang out with the people who looked different on the outside so that it matched what I was also feeling on the inside.

- I wish I would have known that saying no meant I wasn't giving consent for my body to be violated. I wish I would have known in the moment it was rape. I wish I would have told at least one person what had happened. Rape should always be taken seriously. It would have been helpful if I was educated on this subject and knew what someone pressuring me looked like.

As a parent now:

- It's important to be involved in your teen's life. You should know their friends and have them over to your house several times to get to know them. When your instincts tell you something is wrong, trust your gut. It is always best to know the type of individuals your teenager chooses to hang out around because it gives insight into who your teenager is becoming. Teenagers will usually choose to be around like-minded people. Knowing their friends also builds trust, so that if their friends need to come to you with sensitive information, they will feel more inclined too.

- Your teen is like a mini adult, just without the rational thinking skills. Having said that, make your interactions more conversational and not always authoritative. It is our job to prepare them for the adult world and by the time they are teenagers they are only a couple years away from not being a minor anymore. A lot of the parenting and groundwork has been laid out by then and it is now a guidance of decision making to help them along their journey. They will also open up more to you this way.

CHAPTER FOUR

Valentine Nightmare

I would look forward to going to high school every day because I was able to have more freedom and spend time with my friends. I skipped class and hung out with Damien and a couple of others smoking weed in the bathrooms. In early February, Damien was expelled from school for dealing drugs. On February 14, 1999, I decided I would skip school to go hang out with him at his place for the day. I got a ride from one of the guys in a higher grade and was dropped off at Damien's house, just down the street from where my parents lived. Instead of trying to remember and summarize what happened that day, here is a story I wrote on that actual day:

> "Yes," Shannon agreed, as she started to pass her parents on the way up to her room. She was only fifteen years old and yet she felt she already knew the meaning of the word love. Shannon was a bright young lady even though she knew she had made many mistakes in the

past. Everything started when Shannon met Damien, a guy at school. She knew as soon as she saw him that she would connect on a whole different level with him. Her parents on the other hand despised Damien and forbid her to see him—but of course, Shannon had her own plans as she always did.

When Shannon reached her room, she immediately picked up the phone and started to dial. She was very careful of the words she chose as she told Damien the conversation she had just had with her parents about not seeing him anymore. Damien told her that nothing could ever stand in the way of his love for her, which made Shannon feel even more important.

For the next couple of months, she kept her relationship with Damien a secret. She continued to see him by lying to her parents. She would hide their relationship by telling her parents that she was going to a friend's house down the street. Damien would even sneak into her house when her parents had left or weren't paying attention.

During this time, Shannon began to grow even further away from her parents and friends. Eventually Damien was expelled from school and got a full-time job, and they were seldom able to see each other.

On February 14, 1999, Shannon skipped school and got a ride to Damien's home. She never thought she would get caught, but little did she know what was about to happen. At the end of the day, Shannon called her dad, and while pretending to be at school she asked if she could stay late. Her dad knew by this time that Shannon was lying and told her to meet him up at the school in ten minutes. On the way to the school Shannon told Damien everything that was said on the phone with her dad. Damien told her that if her dad hurt her in any way that he was just a phone call away.

As Shannon got out of the car, she kissed Damien good-bye and began proceeding up the long flight of stairs. As she reached her father, he grabbed her by the arm and made her get into his car. He told her that he knew everything and he wanted her to show him where Damien lived. After having her dad drive to a couple of wrong houses because she didn't remember where he lived, Shannon took him to Damien's house.

As they approached the house, Shannon ran out of the car and began to bang on Damien's front door. Once Damien let her in, she quickly ran and hid behind him. Shannon's father yelled at both of them. He asked Damien if he had sex with his daughter, and while Shannon was shaking her head no, Damien told him yes. Shannon's father was furious. Once he finished yelling at Damien, he took Shannon and dragged her out the door. The yelling didn't stop until he finally got Shannon in the car. As soon as she was in the car, Shannon motioned for Damien to call the cops.

As soon as they got home, Shannon's father went into her room and started to throw things out the second-story window. Electronics were flying and hitting the pavement. It was all too much for Shannon to take. She ran to the kitchen and took a handful of aspirin. Based on previous attempts, she knew she hadn't taken nearly enough to kill herself, but her father wouldn't know the difference. To make her father stop, she yelled to him what she had just done and told him there was nothing he could do about it and that it was too late. This got her father to stop throwing her things out the window.

In anger, her father dialed 911. He told them what had happened and within moments the ambulance was at the house. They took Shannon's vitals and spoke to her without her father present. When everything seemed to be okay, Shannon proceeded to tell them that her

father was abusive. She showed them
the bruise on her ankle, which was made
by the car door slamming on it, but the
cops didn't need to know that part. In the
meantime, Shannon's father called her
mother and gave her a head's up on what
was going on. She immediately rushed
home.

I wrote that as a story, but it is exactly what happened on that day. The police told my parents they would need to take me to a psychiatric facility, but my parents refused because that was where I had learned to cut in my previous admission. So, the police made my parents sign a waiver saying they were refusing to send me with them for treatment.

My parents also had to sign a waiver for my psychologist stating they were responsible for my life since they refused to send me to inpatient treatment. My parents felt I was better off at home with them since I had learned unhealthy ways of coping in my previous admittance to the hospital.

Once the police left, my father came into my room and told me that what he was doing was not considered a form of abuse. He was so hurt by the accusations of abuse that he left the house. After a while, things started to settle down, but my life would be again forever changed. What a horrible feeling my dad must have felt when his oldest daughter accused him of such a horrible act. How could I have done something so awful to a father who was forgiving and supportive?

After that my parents began to think about sending me to a home for troubled teens. They had the papers on the counter, and all they had to do was sign on the line. I still don't know why they never sent me, but I was pulled out of the public high school and was homeschooled for half a year by my dad.

My dad would wake me up every day at 8:00 a.m. and make me sit downstairs near his office to do schoolwork. I hated every minute of it. I remember crying almost every day, especially when I would see my friends walking home after school. I felt so confined and trapped. My parents had taken the hinges off my bedroom door and put a tap on our house phone line. I had no privacy and was not allowed to be left alone very often.

My mom has since told me that she and my father went to a spy shop to buy a caller ID system to monitor my incoming and outgoing calls. They said it was one of the strangest stores they had ever stepped foot in, and they felt very out of place.

I found many ways to get around this monitoring. When I wanted to talk to someone my parents did not allow me to talk to, I would call a friend and have them three-way call that person so that my friend's number would show up instead of the main person I wanted to talk to. My friend would usually set the phone down and let me talk to the other person on the three-way call, and we would hang up when we were done. I would also have my friends buy pre-paid phone cards to call me. This way the phone could not be traced by my parents.

CADS

(Cutting, Anxiety, Depression, Suicide)

January 21, 2004

Distorted in the mind,
fogged by a cloud,
Something that can't be defined.
Thoughts that make no sense,
with visions and words
that will make one become tense.
Breathing only gets harder,
anxiety attacks
with chest pains only getting tighter.
The room starts spinning;
The pain deepens within;
The question to be asked...
"When will this end?"
Cutting, it becomes a source;
seeing the blood
only releases the hurt.
And now the end to the beginning,
contemplating suicide
only to attempt it beyond one's mind.
All four in one together;
Cutting, Anxiety, Depression,
    and Suicide,
forever becoming a solution to life.

Without my knowledge, my parents started to do routine checks in my room and go through my bags, trash, mattress, and drawers. My mom would take notes I had written back and forth between my friends and kept track of who was and was not a good influence on me.

One day my dad found a pack of cigarettes in my purse and started yelling at me, saying he couldn't believe I was smoking and that I didn't know what I was doing to myself. I remember thinking how crazy he was because cigarettes should have been the least of his worries. I had started to smoke only when I wasn't able to get my hands on other drugs.

My parents also took away my music. I was listening to a tremendous number of songs about suicide, which only reinforced my thoughts to hurt myself. I felt the words of the songs I was listening to were representative of how I felt. The more songs I listened to, the more engulfed in darkness I became.

I had just gotten my driver's permit and loved to drive, but I couldn't drive without an adult in the car, so my mom realized that driving with me was a good opportunity for her to talk to me. I couldn't exactly go anywhere inside the car. At the same time, my parents knew I needed a professional to talk with, so they put me into counseling. I rarely wanted to open up to my parents, but somehow it seemed easier to talk to someone outside my family.

I started to go back to the other church for youth group on Wednesday nights just to be able to get out of the house. My parents would sit outside the church building every Wednesday to make sure I didn't leave until it was over.

I soon realized the only way I would be able to see Damien and the rest of my friends my parents didn't approve of was to invite them to church. So, I would continue to see Damien at church, and on occasions when my parents weren't sitting outside the doors to the church, we would skip the service and go across the street to Popeye's to hang out. Church soon became my outlet from the prison I was living in at home, and all seemed well to my parents because I wasn't fighting them anymore and was attending church. Little did they know I was continuing to rebel.

One day I asked my parents if one of my friends could come over and spend the night. With reluctance, my parents agreed. They were happy I was finally making some friends and was allowing them to meet the friends.

I brought my friend Tracey home to meet my parents. When Tracey arrived, we walked out to the back porch to say hello. Tracey was dressed in black from head to toe and had many body piercings. She had jet black hair and wore heavy black makeup. I can only imagine what my parents were thinking as she walked up to them and started to talk.

I remember my dad looking straight at her and he said, "Let me ask you a question. You're not, like, going to kill us in the middle of the night, are you?" I was mortified! Looking back now, it was kind-of humorous. Tracey was actually a very nice person, but my parents slept with their door locked that night.

After my parents homeschooled me for my freshman year of high school, they decided to put me back into a private Christian school. I hated that idea but it would be better than being homeschooled. There was a new private Christian school down the road from my house that had just been built. My parents took me to meet the dean of the school, and he gave us an application packet to fill out.

I hated the idea of being put back into a private school, so I refused to complete the application forms. My parents had to fill them out for me and even had to make up my mission statement. The school required each applicant to tell the story of how he or she came to be a Christian, and because I wasn't a Christian yet, my parents had to fill it out for me. Regardless, I was accepted into the school and began my sophomore year there in 2001.

Because it was a private school, I could no longer wear all black. I was required to wear a uniform every day and adhere to very strict rules. I absolutely hated it. I felt I could only be myself on the weekends when I was free to dress and act as I liked.

I didn't make very many friends right away, and I really didn't want to. I would get dropped off for school in the morning, and when I got home, I would immediately go to my room and fall asleep.

During this time, I was also being weaned off my anti-depressant medication and started to have bad withdrawal symptoms. I was always tired and had horrible headaches. I started to turn to other avenues to help with the physical pain. That's when I started popping pills.

I would take anything I could get my hands on, usually some form of pain medication, which helped me get through the long days. I would crave more and more painkillers as the days went on. Eventually, I was dropped to the lowest dose of my antidepressant and stayed on that for the next couple of years.

I still didn't want to eat or gain weight, so at lunch I would sit in the bathroom until it was time for class. When din-ner time came around, I would usually tell my parents that I had either already eaten or had a very late and big lunch. It seemed to work most of the time, but when it didn't and

I was forced to eat, I would revert to throwing it up as soon as I was finished and then making a cut on my body somewhere to remind myself of what I had done. I even started to wear a thick rubber band around my wrist with the words no sugar written in black permanent marker. This too helped to remind me not to eat anything that would cause me to gain weight.

I found many things would help with food cravings. I would train my mind to think I was full every time my stomach would growl and then smoke or take pills to help suppress the hunger feeling. I hated myself and the way I looked.

All Beauty Has Become (2000)

I would have to say one of the major turning points in my life was when I joined my high school cheerleading team. Why in the world would I do that? I wanted to get out of the house as much as possible, and when I heard they were having varsity cheerleading tryouts, I decided I would give it a try. I had been a gymnast when I was younger, so I already knew how to tumble. How hard could it be?

I showed up for tryouts dressed in all black with heavy black makeup and chains hanging from my waist. I was the only one trying out who knew how to tumble, so I made the squad. I cheered for the rest of high school and even some in college. My high school cheerleading coach told me years later that when I first showed up to try out she thought I was crazy and didn't want me on the squad. However, because I was one of the best, she decided to give me a chance. And good thing she did, because I had a lot of fun cheering and even helped our squad win a couple of national and state competitions.

Things I wish I had known:

- I wish I would have known that the damage I did to my body through my eating disorder would cause hormonal issues later in life. Eating disorders effect your metabolism, stress hormones, and fertility. Having an eating disorder effects the hormones responsible for growth and puberty which can result in stunted growth and stunted puberty. It also causes the hormone, cortisol, to increase which can lead to anxiety issues, depression, and sleep problems. I have struggled with many of these issues on and off in my adult life.

- I knew part of the reason I acted the way I did was because I wanted my mom around more. My mom worked a lot and I often felt placed on the back burner. I wish I would have had the coping skills to be able to speak up and tell my mom what I was longing for... her.

- I wish I had the skills to create a closer relationship with my parents. I felt like everything always had to look good on the outside for my parents, and in return the inside connection was pushed aside.

- I wish I knew how much I was hurting my parents and probably even straining their marriage.

As a parent now:

- It's important to teach kids from a young age how to express emotions in a healthy way. If they can safely express how they feel then they will be able to process through those hard feelings and hopefully ask you, their parent, for help when it gets too difficult for them to do it on their own. A great way to help your teenager navigate their feelings is using the feeling wheel. Printing the feeling wheel and allowing your teenager to use it as a reference can help them express their emotions better.

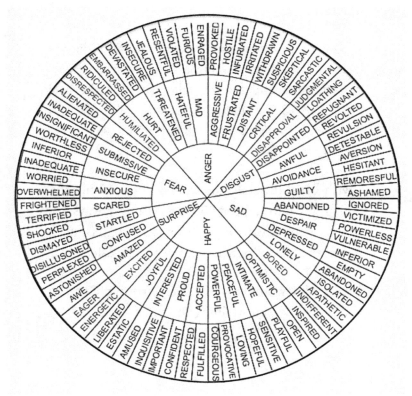

- It's important to let your kids know how impor-tant they are to you and how much they are loved. Go on mini dates with your children and get to know them for who they really are.

- Make it a point to be around your kids and engage in activities they enjoy. In doing this you are showing interest in who they are as individuals. It shows them you care about their identity and respect them for who they are.

- While I understand my dad reacted in anger when he threw my electronics out of the window, this was probably not the best way to respond. It was defi-nitely scary for me as a teenager, especially since my dad and I were already on rocky terms with each other. Looking back, we both needed a cooling off period and space to process what had just happened. After that space was given, we should have reunited to come up with a type of restoration plan.

- When I talked about opening up more while driv-ing with my mother, I now understand the science behind why it worked so well. This is a common technique used in a type of therapy called EMDR (Eye Movement Desensitization and Reprocess-ing). When our eyes are moving back and forth it signals the brain to process what is in the sub-conscious. When driving or walking, we are con-stantly looking around. This helps us to process information in our brains and sometimes talk about what we are processing. So, the next time you want someone to open up and communicate their thoughts and emotions, take them for a drive or go for a walk.

CHAPTER FIVE

Turning Point

My life started to turn around in a more positive direction. I continued going to church with my parents on a regular basis. One evening the pastor asked if anyone would like to get to know Jesus on a more personal level. He invited those who did to meet an usher at the front of the room. Having sat through many of these services with me, my parents didn't think I would ever come to know Christ—but on this night something was different. I felt a tugging feeling, and something told me it was time. I stood up from my seat and moved out into the aisle. My parents thought I was going to run away during the service, but instead I began walking toward the front of the room.

After twenty minutes of talking with a nice lady, I walked out to meet my family. My mom was stunned when she saw me walking toward her. As I reached my family, I leaned in and told them I had accepted Christ into my life and asked Him to be my personal Savior.

I was now a Christian. My parents couldn't believe what they heard. I made sure they knew it was my decision and that I still had a lot I would need to work through. My

parents were so happy at that moment they hugged me for
what seemed like forever.

Daddy

August 24, 2000

Daddy,
I see Thee in white
Sitting on Thy throne;
Angels to Thy right
and the devil below.
Daddy,
Why a happy face?
For when Thy eyes look upon me,
they should see such a disgrace.
Daddy,
Thy heart is pure
But blood drips down
for my cure.
Daddy,
Why?
Help me to see,
Why You suffered
to set me free.

Temptation Is Fearful

June 10, 2003

Help me, Lord,
I'm crying to Thee;
I've made mistakes
And was blind as can be.
I pray, forgive me
For what I have done;
Cleanse my soul
From being the awful one.
I could have helped myself,
And the path was clear;
And now because of temptation
all I have is fear.
You are the only one
That can save me now;
Cleanse my heart and soul
and to You I bow.
I need my life back;
I can't live knowing,
Because of my sin
Everything I have is gone.
You are the sovereign One,
and to You I pray,
Give me a second chance
That I may live to see another day.

I continued seeing a counselor, and although I didn't stop smoking or popping pills right away, I did gradually begin to cut down on my use. I started to date a guy named Thomas who was a year ahead of me in school, and my parents loved him. We dated for three and a half years, and I owe him a tremendous amount of thanks. He really helped me break some bad habits. And, even better, my parents trusted him, so I was able to get out of the house for longer periods of time.

I told him a lot about my past, and he did everything he could to try to get me back on the right path. He encouraged me to avoid rock music when I was around him because listening to it would usually make me feel depressed. He always made sure we were hanging out with friends who had a positive influence on us and that we did activities that were safe and acceptable. I'm not going lie—I would steal a couple of his rock CDs every once in a while, and listen to them, but for the most part he was a great influence on me and helped me transform into the person I am today.

I eventually stopped wearing all black all the time and quit smoking. I also stopped changing my hair color and decided to stick with blonde hair. I grew closer to my family and would attend our yearly family vacations again. By my senior year I had stopped cutting, quit smoking, quit popping pills, and began to wear more colorful clothes. I was transforming from a dark phase and into a happier, lighter stage of my life.

Although I didn't necessarily enjoy my high school years because I ended up back in private school, these years were the transition period in my life. My family made it a point to take control of the situation and monitored me more closely. I was surrounded by positive influences, including the music I listened to, the movies I watched, the people I was allowed to hang out with, and the clothes I was allowed to wear.

After I graduated from high school in 2003, I decided it was time for me to leave the house. I moved to Jacksonville,

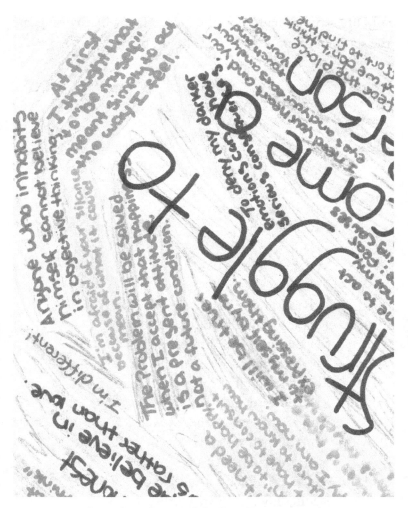

Struggle to Become My Own Person (2001)

Florida with a good friend and attended college at the University of North Florida for the next four years.

I started to gain a lot of my freedom back and even began to feel better about myself. I still wrote a lot of poetry, but instead of always writing about death, I wrote more about daily life struggles and love. For once, I was discovering my true self—not who I thought I should be.

Changing Paths

February 4, 2003

So many decisions come my way,
so many choices to make it this day.
My mind is fogged,
My head aches;
I think to myself,
What about mistakes?
I wonder what will happen
When I finally leave this place;
I want to think I won't be a disgrace.
Starting over is what I have to do;
Lead a different life
Then the one that hurts me through
    and through.
New friends will come my way,
And maybe I won't have to pretend
what I do now to fit in.
A couple of months and I'm on my own,
leading my life down a different road.

I did great in college and loved being away from Orlando. I swore to myself I would never return to what I thought of as a "God-awful" city. I finally understood the reason I went through so much pain.

I pursued a degree in psychology and was able to help many other young girls who were going through something similar to what I experienced. I knew this was my calling.

I cheered for a year while in college, gained some weight, joined a sorority, and became a part of the psychology club. Don't get me wrong—I partied a lot and skipped a lot of classes to go to the beach, but I felt a lot better about myself and my life.

I graduated college in 2007 with a Bachelor of Science in psychology and a minor in sociology. I now hold a master's degree in mental health counseling from Nova Southeastern University. I know, I just said I hated Orlando, but I moved back because I met the love of my life!

I am about to tell you about my life as it is today, so if all you wanted to read about was the hard times I experienced when I was younger, then put the book down now or turn to Chapter 7, A Voice. However, I believe it is important to share this new chapter in my life with you so you can see how far I have come. I hope it also instills a little glimpse of hope for you and your family's future.

In a Man...

February 4, 2003

I want a man who loves me,
someone to trust and to hold me.
I want a man who knows me,
who is not afraid to understand
the trials of my past.
I want romance and laughter,
and a long life to look after.
I want a shoulder to cry on
when I'm in need;
I want someone to talk to, please.
I want to be comfortable
and not have to look my best;
I want him to love me through every test.
When I don't look my best
and it's all because of PMS,
I want to know he won't judge me,
but take me in his arms and
forever love me.
I want to know it's going to last forever,
And I want to hear him say,
He loves me every day of the year.

Things I wish I had known:

- I wish I had known my life was going to be great, but I'm glad I went through these trying times because they made me the person I am today.

As a parent now:

- Our kids are going to struggle in life. It is our job to raise them with a positive foundation so that when they do struggle, they will have that foundation to come back to. I also believe in early intervention for young kids. We need to teach our children a variety of positive coping skills.

CHAPTER SIX

The Story of Our Love

Steve was born in Miami, Florida on March 30, 1979. He was raised by his wonderful mother and grandmother. Steve has one younger sibling, with whom he is very close. Because his father was in and out of his life, Steve quickly took on the role of the protector in his family. He started his own business when he was fourteen-years-old and continued to cultivate other areas of interests throughout the years. Now he is a general contractor and doing very well.

He bought his first home at age twenty-one and lived there with his sister and the young woman who was his fiancée at the time. He had been engaged to her for a couple years but felt something was missing.

That's when I came along. You already know a lot of my story. I was born in Orlando, Florida, on March 28, 1985. I was raised by my mother and father and am very close to my grandmother. I have one younger sibling, Stacey, who just so happens to have the same first and middle name as Steve's sister. I attended private Christian schools for most of my education and graduated with a bachelor's degree from a public university—the University of North Florida—in May

2007. I also graduated with my master's degree in mental health counseling from Nova Southeastern University.

I have always believed things happen for a reason and that God has chosen a soulmate for every person. Having said that, let me tell you the story of how Steve and I met.

It all began with my dad, a group of his friends, and a ski trip. Ever since I was a young girl, my family has always enjoyed skiing. My dad and a group of men even started the Orlando Ski Club. They met once a year for a week in January to go on a guys' ski trip to Utah. A week later, the women and children would fly out and meet the men for another week on the slopes. For a couple of years, my best friend, Emily, and I would meet our dads in Utah to go skiing.

In 2006, the guys decided to do a combined ski trip with everyone together. I was still in college and home on break, so I could go. Emily, however, was not able to go, and I was very reluctant to go by myself—but I decided to join them anyway. My dad told me we would share a vehicle with his friend, who was my dentist, Dr. Ross, and someone named Steve, whom I assumed was the same age as my dad. The night before the trip, I was very ill. In fact, I almost didn't go—but something pushed me to go.

Very early the next morning, my dad and I drove to the Orlando airport. As we were standing at the gate getting ready to board the flight to Utah, Steve walked up to my dad and shook his hand. He was definitely not my dad's age. In fact, he was around my age. Before he could even introduce himself, I immediately thought, *this is the guy I am going to marry.* As he shook my hand and introduced himself, I tried to stop the thought that was going through my mind and snap out of it, but I knew there was something different about him.

Somehow, we both forgot the fact that we had significant others back home. My dad even kept mentioning something about Steve's wife. I went through the entire first day in Utah thinking Steve was married and there was no chance of anything ever turning into a relationship. Then later that day, Dr. Ross tried to put my dad in his place by saying Steve wasn't married, only engaged. By this time, I was really confused.

The next night we went out to get some barbeque for dinner. No one seemed to be talking, so I decided to use the opportunity to get some information out of Steve. I needed better clarification into his love life. I looked up at Steve, who was sitting across from me and said, "Wait a minute. You're not married and you don't have a ring on your finger. So, what are you?"

As you can imagine, Steve was completely floored! "Shannon, you're being rude!" my dad said. "Stop

asking so many questions."

Dr. Ross, however, darted right in there. "Yeah, Steve. What are you two?"

Steve thought about it for a minute or two and then said, "Well, she's my girlfriend." He went on to explain that he wasn't very happy in his relationship and had a lot to think about.

The next morning Steve was very quiet when he came down for breakfast. When I asked him what was wrong, he replied that he wasn't happy with his fiancée and was going to call things off with her. He had been thinking of calling off his relationship for the last couple of years but was comfortable and that was why he hadn't done it yet. I was so excited, but I tried to keep my face from showing it.

The following days of skiing were great. Steve and I would try to sit next to each other on the lift or at dinner so that we could talk. I could tell he was nervous, although I was still unsure if he was really interested in me. Maybe he thought I was too young for him. I was still in college and in a sorority, and he was working full-time running his personal business, so I was in a different phase of life than he was.

The evening before we were to head back to Orlando, Steve and I decided to build a snowman. Dr. Ross said it couldn't be done with the type of snow that had fallen—it was too dry—so of course we decided to show him! In fact, the snow was so dry that it took us two hours just to get the first two balls of the snowman together, but it was a great time to get to know each other better. We both learned a lot and realized we had more in common than anyone else we had ever met.

It was a great bonding experience and we were falling for each other. After two hours, it was time to go to dinner. When my dad saw we hadn't gotten too far on building our snowman, he laughed and popped an orange road cone on top of the snowman for his head. It was great!

The last night of our vacation, I decided to give Steve my contact information. I handed him a piece of paper with my number, email, and AIM information (AOL Instant Messenger; dating myself). In my mind I was hoping he would want to call me for a date or something, but I told him if he ever needed to talk or just wanted to hang out sometime, he should give me a call.

The next morning, we boarded the plane to head back to Orlando. We flirted with each other the entire plane ride. It was fun, but inside my heart was breaking because the next day I would head back to Jacksonville and I didn't know if we would ever see each other again.

As we got off the plane in Orlando, we headed down to the luggage claim. Steve and I stayed a little behind my dad and Dr. Ross and very nonchalantly Steve handed me his business card with all his information. I didn't really know what to think except, *at least I have his number now*. There was no guarantee he would ever call.

Steve's ride was running late and I really wanted to drive him home, but I knew it probably wouldn't be appropriate since his fiancée would be there. It wasn't long before my mom came to pick up Dad and me. She gave me a big hug and suddenly it was time to say good-bye to Steve.

That night I stayed in Orlando at my parents' house. The next morning, I would have to drive back to Jacksonville for classes. I just couldn't help myself that night, so I decided to text Steve and ask if he got home all right. I never received an answer, so I wrote him an email letting him know what a great time I had and how happy I was that I met him. The next morning, I got an email back from him, and that's when the communication really started.

He told his fiancée that he didn't think their relationship was meant to be and she moved out shortly thereafter. For the next couple of days, we would continue to write to each other. Eventually we started to talk on the phone for hours each night. I grew farther and farther apart from my boyfriend at the time and eventually called things off.

One day I invited Steve to come see me in Jacksonville. He was so nervous but did come for a visit. We had lunch at Angie's Subs (he was so nervous he couldn't eat). In the following weeks, Steve and I continued to talk and learn more about each other. From that day on, we didn't spend one weekend apart. It was challenging driving back and forth from Orlando to Jacksonville, but we were both so in love with each other that it didn't matter.

Steve and I loved going to a restaurant on the beach called Sunny Caribbean. We would sit outside and eat while listening to the ocean. One night after we ate, we decided to take a walk on the beach. After walking for a little bit, we sat on top of a lifeguard tower and listened to the ocean waves. The sky was dark and cloudy and not a soul was around. Steve put his arms around me and held me tight. He looked into my eyes and said, "I had really pictured this different. I wanted to tell you this under the stars on a perfect night, but I love you. I love you so much!"

I was so taken back that I didn't know what to say. After the shock subsided, I immediately said, "I love you too!" Right as we said those three words, I looked up in the sky to see thousands of stars shining right above us. One minute it was so cloudy and the next minute the stars were illuminating the sky. It was like a sign we were really meant to be together forever.

It took a while for my dad to warm up to Steve. We were six years apart in age and my dad really couldn't get past the age difference. Our first Christmas together was wonderful—until the day after Christmas. I got into a tiff with my parents and as a result we did not talk with them for months.

I went through a lot of counseling, and after months of not talking, we were all finally able to come to terms with each other. Steve and my dad had lunch together and talked things through, and the relationship between all of us started over. It would have been so easy for Steve to walk away. Instead, he stuck by me through everything. He never once said it was too tough. He showed me unconditional love.

I graduated from college in May 2007. My entire family drove up to attend the ceremony, and the next day I moved back to Orlando. That night my family took Steve and me out to dinner at the Cheesecake Factory to celebrate and then we went back to the house to open gifts. My parents gave me a book of photographs of New York City. Finally, I realized they were giving me not just a book—but a trip to New York. My parents and I would leave the following weekend, which was perfect since Steve was going to be in Texas for a business trip.

As soon as we arrived in New York, Steve's good friend, Phil, who is like a brother to him, and Phil's girlfriend, Kristine, met us at the airport. They had both taken time off work to show us around the big city for the day. And it was a long day! Phil took us everywhere possible and stopped at every stand to get something to eat. The guy has an appetite like I have never seen.

They first took us into Brooklyn to get the best pizza ever. Then we headed into the city for some sightseeing. Toward the end of the day, my parents said our last stop would be the Empire State Building. I really wanted to save it for the next day because I was exhausted, but everyone insisted we do it that day. It didn't take too long to get to the top, and once we were up there, the sight was amazing.

I started to walk around the platform at the top of the building to see the city from every angle when my dad came running up to me. "Look there!" he said pointing over the edge. I couldn't see what he was pointing at, but he seemed so excited, so I just kept looking. I felt a tap on my shoulder but didn't turn around because I didn't want to miss whatever my dad was so excited about.

After the second tap, I turned around—and there was Steve. He handed me a rose, and before I could say anything, he got down on one knee right in front of me. My mind couldn't wrap around what he was doing, and I kept trying to pull him to his feet. Suddenly I spotted a small box in his hand and I realized exactly what was happening. I was so shocked I could barely hear the words coming from his mouth as he asked me to marry him. I started crying and replied yes, but it was so soft that no one heard me. Finally, someone shouted, "Did she say yes?" This time I said, "Yes!" really loud.

I looked up and there was a crowd around us. They were all taking our pictures. We felt like celebrities. The parents of Steve's best friend were there along with my parents and Phil and Kristine. It was perfect! The celebration moved to Brooklyn where we had a wonderful engagement party at an Italian restaurant.

After dinner Steve told me how he pulled off the surprise. I told him I had gotten a little suspicious about his supposed business trip to Texas because he wasn't giving me much information and hadn't asked me to come along. He knew I was a snooper and would try to find out the truth if he was hiding something, so he got my parents in on the task of trying to throw me off. They kept talking about how hot it would be in Texas and even gave him suggestions of where to go for good Mexican food. Steve even went so far as to leave a day before I did—except he actually flew to New York. He really did a great job of covering his steps.

After we got back from New York, the wedding planning started. I can't believe how much work it is to plan a wedding, especially without a wedding planner.

I already had an idea of the kind of wedding I wanted and started putting together an organized notebook. At first, Steve and I decided on a small wedding in a chapel in downtown Orlando, but as the plans started getting underway, we realized it was going to be bigger than we had originally thought, so we had to move it to a bigger location. It seemed as if I had countless appointments with various vendors and had to make many decisions fast. I wanted it to be a day to remember just as any bride would.

Uniting Our Love

December 30, 2007

The day we dream of,
a girl's fantasy;
A perfect walk
Centered on me.
Hours of planning,
nights of dreams;
Sleepless again,
forever it seems.
Counting the days,
it's approaching fast;
Together with my honey,
Forever at last.
Dressed in white,
Sheer across my face;
A princess A-lined dress,
Beaded down with lace.
Pearly white strands
Draped around my neck;
Not failing with detail,
Down to every last speck.
Together at the altar hand in hand;
Waves of emotion as here we stand.
A love so strong bound with God;
Family and friends
Sharing in our love.
Tears of happiness
Stream down my face;
Together we say, "I do."
With the exchanging of rings.
Married at last,

Headed for our honeymoon;
Leaving for our cruise
And later to kiss beneath the moon.

The evening before our wedding, we had our rehearsal dinner at Dubsdread Country Club in Orlando. It was so great to have our closest friends and family together the night before our big day. The morning of January 5, 2008, I woke up early because I had a hard time sleeping the night before. My dad had gone to breakfast with Steve (he was so nervous he didn't eat a bite!) and a couple of the guys to help calm him down. My mom made my favorite breakfast: blueberry waffles. I almost never get so nervous that I can't eat, but that particular morning, I couldn't bring myself to put a bite into my mouth.

Kathy, my mom's good friend, came over early to help my mom with her makeup and dress. My bridesmaids were all at the salon getting their hair done, and Steve went shooting with the guys. So that left me all alone with butterflies in my tummy and hours to spare before having to get ready for my wedding.

When I get even a little bit nervous there is only one thing to help calm me down: shopping! So, I went to Target and bought a clutch and a new pair of silver shoes for our honeymoon. Those made me feel a lot better. Early in the afternoon I went to get my hair done and meet up with my bridesmaids. A little later Kathy came to pick us up to take us to the church. We were a little bit late, and I later found out that Steve asked someone to make sure I was still coming.

The church was beautiful! As I finished getting ready, many of my close friends and family came in to see me. I kept asking how Steve was doing because I thought he was going to be very nervous. He hates to get in front of a large group of people, and he was about to stand in front of almost 200 guests. Surprisingly, I was told that he wasn't nervous at all and couldn't wait to get the wedding started.

The ceremony started at 5:00 p.m. Right before we were about to begin it started to sprinkle outside. I was so happy because I heard it was good luck if it rains on your wedding day. We all lined up as the seating of the family started. I saw the groomsmen standing at the front of the church and then I saw Steve. I was finally about to marry the man of my dreams.

The wedding party started to walk down the aisle. When it came time for my dad to walk me to the altar, he started to tear up. He told me he thought I was doing the right thing by marrying Steve and that I looked beautiful. It was great to have my dad by my side on one of the most important days of my life. As we approached the altar, the pastor started to speak. When he asked who gives this lady away, my dad replied, "Her mother and I do." Steve was supposed to come and take my hand from my dad, but he forgot and my dad had to motion for him. It was quite humorous.

Immediately following the wedding, we took more pictures and headed off to our reception at the Orlando Country Club. Steve and I had prepared a surprise choreographed dance for our first dance together. We had practiced for months and finally learned how to do the fox trot. When it came time for our first dance, Steve was so nervous he could barely talk to me. We danced to "New York, New York" by Frank Sinatra. The guests were hooting and hollering and really enjoyed our performance. Later we enjoyed speeches by my sister, Steve's best man, and my dad. They were tear-jerkers! The reception lasted well into the night. In fact, the DJ had to coax people off the dance floor because it was getting so late. He sent all our guests outside the country club to get ready to send us off with sparklers and bubbles. While they did that, Steve and I had one last slow, romantic dance together with no one around.

Next thing I knew we were running out of the country club and into a limo. (We had to turn around and go back to the country club after we took off because Steve forgot his wallet and keys)! January 5, 2008, we started our life together as Mr. and Mrs. Steven Rowell.

The next day we took off to Miami to catch a cruise to the southern Caribbean. We boarded the ship and headed for our room, which was decorated with colorful balloons, banners, and a cake. My parents surprised us with a nice bottle of wine and chocolate-covered strawberries. The cruise was so much fun, and we were able to visit many unique places. We also had a great view from our balcony so at night we would have a glass of wine and sit outside. We spent a week on the cruise, and when we got back, we moved all my belongings into Steve's house (now our house) and began our life journey together.

It's now thirteen years later and Steve and I are still very happily married. We have four amazing children and love living life to its fullest.

CHAPTER SEVEN

A Voice

It was certainly a whirlwind year. In a span of about eight months, I graduated, moved back to Orlando, got engaged, planned my wedding, got married, started my master's program, and started a new job. Guess what the job was? Working in a psychiatric facility as a mental health technician. I worked in an inpatient unit with some of the worst mental health cases, and I enjoyed every minute of it. Not only was I able to learn many new and exciting things working within the mental health field, but I was also able to help the population I longed to serve based on everything I had gone through myself. At times the days drained me, but I reminded myself that God had placed me there for a reason and every day made a difference when I was able to help others.

I worked there for more than a year and created a group therapy program for the patients. I was even able to facilitate some of the groups. This experience reaffirmed my desire to work within the mental health field.

After a year I decided it would be more beneficial to work for the same organization but in the fundraising department, which allowed me to help raise money and awareness for the behavioral health center. Around then I was working full-time, had just graduated with my master's degree in mental health counseling, and was finishing my practicum working with sexual abuse victims.

Another huge change happened at that time: Steve and I were expecting our first baby boy, Preston Marshall Rowell. We were thrilled to become new parents. I hope I will be able to help my children through every one of life's trials as others have helped me in the past.

I would not have been able to do any of this with such a strong passion if I hadn't traveled the road, I did. Every experience I had was a divine intervention from God to guide me down a path to help others. I am so thankful I had the love and support of my family and friends to get me through my troubled years. I can only pray that God will continue to use me for His kingdom to continue to help others who are struggling.

As I started my journey, I had not yet accepted Christ as my Lord and Savior. In fact, I was involved in the opposite of what He wanted for me. I have been down a road of pure evil and destruction, but through the grace of our Lord and Savior I was saved and am now His daughter. I have surrendered my life to Christ, knowing He allowed me to continue down a crooked path for a purpose. God judged it better to bring good out of evil than to not let evil happen. "I consider that our present sufferings are not worth comparing with the glory that will be revealed in us" (Rom. 8:18). A true benefit to having suffered is being able to help others going through something similar.

Every life has meaning and a purpose. Each one of us is unique and has his or her own set of strengths that can be used for the greater good of society. I believe everything happens for a reason. If we are going through hard times, it will make us stronger, and we will learn how to handle future situations. When bad things happen, although it may be unpleasant and hurtful, God will not give us more than we can handle. If we have faith and trust, we can get through anything.

You may be experiencing something like what I have gone through. Perhaps you feel completely hopeless. I am here to tell you where there is pain, there is hope! We may not always know or understand what or why we are going through tough times, but reaching for help and support can help get you through your time of need.

For years I have done a tremendous amount of soul-searching and self-discovery. I believe I was put on this earth to serve Christ and others through Him. I believe His purpose for my life was predetermined to prepare me to help those who do not have a voice. He has allowed me to endure circumstances involving mental health issues so that I would gain experience and understanding for my journey to becoming a mental health professional. My life is a gift, and I have been given an open book to write from beginning to end. Life is like drawing without an eraser, and each stage brings new and exciting challenges with opportunities for positive change.

Many of my personality traits came from my family. My mother has always been a hardworking woman and has climbed her way up the executive ladder. She has instilled in me the drive to always strive for excellence, even in the worst circumstances. My father always taught me persistence and perseverance are key skills to have throughout life. I am very persistent and love a challenge. I have formed my identity from the assets my parents have instilled in me. I know there is no one just like me, and therefore I must strive to do the best I can to touch others' lives in a positive manner.

I want to make a difference as a mental health counselor. I plan to do this by reducing stigma, raising awareness and funds for the mental health field, creating a better environment within the inpatient setting, and inspiring the lives of those seeking counseling. In 2010 I became a licensed mental health counselor and started working in the field. My dream came true in 2011 when I opened my own private practice, Perfectly Imperfect Counseling.

I have gained various strengths and insights based on the many challenges I have experienced thus far. Once a young girl who was naïve and dependent, I have grown into a woman with confidence and passion for life. I have learned how it feels to experience pain and to give pain, how to love others unconditionally and to maintain a desire to enrich the lives of those I encounter. I know I make a wonderful wife, mother, sister, granddaughter, and counselor. I will give my all until the day I am no longer called to.

A NOTE TO THOSE HURTING

I know you're searching for something more in this world. I know it hurts emotionally and physically. I know you feel alone and think no one understands what you are going through. I know…I was there!

I don't want my story to sound as if I went through so much horror and then suddenly, I was cured, because that would be inaccurate. I must honestly tell you that although I have come a long way from where I started, I still struggle mildly today. I am no longer on medication for depression; however, I occasionally struggle with panic attacks when I become overwhelmed or stressed. I always have an anti-anxiety medication on hand just in case I ever need it, and occasionally I do. That is okay.

I also struggle with my appearance from time to time. I am now at a healthy weight, but often have distorted thoughts of my body image. I just keep reminding myself that I am beautiful and don't need to go to extremes to be thin. I must be careful when I do go on diets because my old habits quickly come rushing back. There are times when I look in the mirror and think I am extremely overweight, but instead of engaging in unhealthy behaviors, I tell my husband my thoughts so that I can receive his support.

As far as cutting, I have done a complete turnaround. The scars I have are barely visible. I think I am really the only one who can see them because I am the one who made them. Although I no longer cut, there are times when life can get me very down, and immediately my thoughts turn to what I knew. I know this is something I will continue to battle in my thoughts, but I also know I have overcome the physical aspect and only faint scars remain.

Other past experiences have left me. I am no longer into alcohol, drugs, or witchcraft. I try to keep myself from falling back into my old ways by telling my story. It helps to reinforce how far I have come by saying it aloud. My past will always be something I cannot change, but my future holds promising experiences to help others. I know I will make it my mission to be the voice for those who do not feel they have a voice.

I encourage everyone to speak with a counselor at some point in their life, and you are no different. Please know there is help and there is hope. Hold on to the little bit of wonder inside you telling you that there is something better out there, and then search for it. If you are experiencing the same things, I did, I advise you to fight against the hopeless feelings that threaten to overwhelm you. Try to find one positive glimpse of hope to hold on to. "And hope maketh not ashamed" (Rom. 5:5a, kjv).

Looking back, I believe if I would have disclosed the many experiences I had as a child, I would have been diagnosed with Post-Traumatic Stress Disorder (PTSD). This is an important concept to understand because you or someone you know may have PTSD without realizing, and it is extremely vital to seek professional help.

PTSD occurs when someone has experienced a traumatic event involving actual or threatened death or injury, or a threat to one's integrity followed by intense fear or helplessness, such as being raped. This is according to the DSM V, the diagnostic manual for mental disorders. There are many characteristics involved with PTSD. Some of the ones I experienced were distressing memories of my rape experience, flashbacks, and nightmares.

If you have been exposed to a traumatic event and think you may be experiencing some of the symptoms of PTSD, I encourage you to seek professional help. I did not disclose being raped until seven years after it had happened. If I would have sought help earlier, I could have prevented the longevity of the symptoms I was experiencing.

Surround yourself with others who are the opposite of how you are feeling. Don't let yourself be alone. Reach for something more and explore what Christ has in store for you. Believe me, it's something big!

A NOTE TO PARENTS AND LOVED ONES OF THOSE HURTING

There are certain indicators that you can look for if you suspect your teen is struggling.

There must be a balance between tough love and providing comfort. We all make mistakes, but I would like to share with you a few things my parents did right when going through this journey with me.

I firmly believe it is important to shut out all negative influences. What I mean by this is to limit the forces that go against your family values. My parents did well by trying to limit my contact with my negative peer group. Those friends taught me a lot of what I knew. I was getting mixed messages from what my friends believed and what my parents had brought me up to believe. That's why it is important to watch and listen.

Watch out for changes in behavior and attitude in your teen. You can see this in many ways. You may start to see a change in the friends your teen chooses. They may stop hanging out with their regular group of friends and choose another group, such as friends who are older than they are. You may see a negative shift in mood during this time. Their mood may go from pleasant to depressed or even defiant. If a difference or fluctuation in mood is evident, it is important for you to assess for suicidal ideations and self-injurious behaviors.

Listen for statements such as, "I hate my life and don't want to live anymore." If you hear this, take it seriously and make it a priority to have a conversation with your teen to see what is really going on.

Keep an eye on cough, cold, and prescription medications in your home. Self-injurious behaviors may include self-medicating through medications already in your house. Also watch the way your teen dresses. Adolescents who cut themselves tend to wear long-sleeved shirts and dress in colors that reflect their mood, such as black for depression.

If you suspect cutting, nonchalantly check your teen's arms, legs, thighs, stomach, wrists, and ankles. These are just a few common places found in those who cut. Adolescents who cut themselves will most likely have scars from picking off the scabs. Cutting usually occurs when one is feeling so low that they use cutting to release the internal pain they are feeling.

If you suspect your teen is engaging in self-injurious behaviors, do not panic, at least not in front of them. Instead, take a calm approach by explaining that you understand they are hurting and in pain. Explain that you can understand how harming themselves is a release of that pain, but that you are concerned about them and would like them to pursue, with your help, professional mental health services.

If you are close to someone who cuts, I encourage you not to display disappointment or feelings of disgust. Instead love them where they are and show them you don't look down on them or think they are weird because they have chosen to cope through cutting. The last thing you want to do is make them think they are not normal. I am not saying you must condone the action, but they will most likely continue to cut whether you like it or not.

My mom showed me she loved me unconditionally when she personally rubbed oil on my scars. She stayed by my side even when it looked as if there was truly no hope left. I would have to compare her actions to the story in the Bible when Jesus showed the full extent of His love by washing His disciples' feet before His final hour (see John 13:2-4).

Jesus, the Son of God, should have had His feet washed by His disciples. Instead, He showed that love is laying down one's life. Loving completely means to love to the end of one's life. As a teenager, I should have been the one showing respect to my mother. Instead, my mother showed me that despite her disapproval of my choice to harm myself, she was still able to love me through it all. A family photo hangs in my parent's house, and if you look closely, you can see the outline of the misspelled word "Vampire" that I had carved in my arm. Yet she took care of me so that the physical scars would become less visible. To this day it is hard to tell that I was ever a cutter.

As you watch for changes in mood, remember that adolescents strive for independence and will push you away every chance they get. They may even say hurtful statements directed toward you such as, "I hate you." It is important for parents and/or caregivers to realize these statements are usually made to be interpreted in the opposite of their meaning. Since your teenage child feels comfortable around you, they also feel safe saying hurtful words to you (to those they love/respect). Adolescents may push you away, but inside they are crying for your support and help. Do not leave your teen during this emotional time. Instead let them know you are with them physically and emotionally. Let them know you will never give up on them.

Another area to "listen and watch" are phone calls, texting, and social media. Although my parents didn't have to worry too much about my internet use because it wasn't as popular as it is today, I strongly suggest parents monitor their children's social networks online. It never feels good to have "big brother" constantly watching over you, but when you are in this type of situation, I believe it is best to know who your child is conversing with daily.

This also applies to searching your teen's room. Based on experience, I would highly suggest if you are going to search through their room that you not make it known to them. The reasons for this are simple. The less they know that you know about their life, the easier it will be to find information. For instance, if I knew my parents were regularly searching my room, I would have distrusted them even more than I already did and would have come up with new and innovative ways to hide things from them.

Pay attention to the times your child does talk to you. When I got my driver's permit, my mother drove with me wherever I went and used that opportunity to talk with me— and to listen to what I was saying.

Another important note is to pick and choose your battles. It was important for my parents to limit my contact with outside negative influences, but fighting about the clothes I wore was not a battle my parents decided to pick. I usually wore all black every day (and honestly still do because I like it). By my parents allowing me to continue this trend, they were giving me the opportunity to have my own identity.

This gave me an outlet to express myself when other outlets were taken away. It also gave me a sense of control over who I was.

Finally, as parents remember that you have the spiritual authority over your children. Pray for them and over them for their guidance and protection. My mother would sneak into my room at night while I was sleeping and place her hand on my feet and pray over me. I can't stress how important this is. If you do nothing else, pray. Your child doesn't even have to know you are praying for/over them. In fact, I probably wouldn't do it at a time they are aware because it may drive them even farther away if they are not accepting of it.

Don't underestimate the power of the prayers as a parent. Jesus said, "Behold, I give you the authority to trample on serpents and scorpions, and over all the power of the enemy, and nothing shall by any means hurt you" (Luke 10:19 nkjv). As much as your child may wish for you not to help them, there is something to be said for the parent who exerts control over a difficult situation involving his or her child. Every parent has the right to know who his or her child is hanging out with, the type of music they are listening to, or the television shows they are watching, what applications they are using on their phones, and where they are at all times. It becomes problematic when parents know their child is involved in unhealthy things yet choose to live in denial and not act.

Parents, you do have legal rights over your children who are under eighteen years of age. When all else fails and you are in a crisis, there are two main legal options you should be aware of.

A Florida Baker Act should be initiated when your teen is displaying suicidal and/or homicidal ideations. If you believe your child is in serious danger of harming themselves or other people and you feel action should be initiated immediately, you can initiate the Baker Act. You can do this by calling law enforcement and explaining the suicidal and/or homicidal ideations your child is displaying. Law enforcement will pick up your child and bring them to the nearest Baker Act receiving facility where they can be held for a psychological evaluation for up to seventy-two hours. Advantages of the Baker Act are immediate safety, psychological assessment, medical evaluation, intervention, and possible entry to group or individual therapy.

The disadvantages of the Baker Act are your child will most likely be placed in handcuffs to be transported to the facility. This is due to liability and the safety of the officer at hand. The other disadvantage can be that your child may pick up other bad habits from other patients in the facility.

I personally would try to voluntarily commit my child into a private facility before initiating a Baker Act. These types of facilities are a lot nicer and are taken better care of for their patients.

The next option available to you is the Marchman Act. The Marchman Act is initiated for individuals in need of treatment for substance abuse. By law, a minor is able to seek treatment for substance abuse without the permission of a parent or caregiver. However, an involuntary admission for treatment through the Marchman Act can be initiated when an individual is impaired by a substance and has lost control or is threatening to inflict harm on themselves or others.

To initiate the Marchman Act, you should file a Marchman Act petition with the court, and within ten days a hearing will be set. A judge will decide if the person in question will need to be placed involuntarily in a substance-abuse treatment facility. If a judge decides it is best for involuntary admission to a treatment facility, a law officer, in regular street clothes, will be sent to detain the individual for treatment. A person may be held for assessment and observation in a substance-abuse treatment facility for up to five days.

The Baker Act and the Marchman Act are great resources for you to utilize in crisis with your troubled teen or child. Please research the above options to make the best-informed decision.

FRIEND TO FRIEND

If you are a friend of someone going through a difficult time, signs may be more evident for you. Your friends will most likely disclose their feelings and thoughts more readily to you than they would to their parents. They may show you their scars from injuring themselves or tell you they are feeling depressed.

Take these signs seriously, and seek help from a trusted adult. If you can, do not break your friend's trust by going behind their backs, but instead explain to your friends that you care about them and want to be with them every step of the way. If they know they will have a friend with them through this difficult time, they will be more prone to receiving help.

PARENT TO PARENT

I asked my mother to write something that would help other parents who are dealing with the same issues that she and my dad dealt with.

—⁂—

Having read Shannon's story, you might find it helpful to hear about my journey as a parent going through this very difficult time with a child, I loved dearly but who had become a stranger to me. I hope that what I learned in trying to help Shannon will be beneficial to you. What I will share with you is, of course, just a reflection of my own experience. Every situation is different.

If you face a similar ordeal with your child, the first thing I would say to you is never give up hope. During these trying times your child needs you more than ever. Hope is the beacon of light amid these darkest of times. This is what I have learned as a parent in trying to help Shannon.

As Shannon described, she was a wonderfully happy, easy-going child. My husband and I raised Shannon and her sister with the Christian values and beliefs that we both share. They were involved in Sunday school, church, and youth group, and they both went to Christian schools. As I learned, this is not an insurance policy that will keep your child from straying off the right path. Yet, although Shannon strayed from these core beliefs, I believe the Christian foundation she had growing up eventually helped her turn her life around. The Bible speaks about this in Proverbs 22:6: "Train a child in the way he should go, and when he is old, he will not turn from it."

The first sign of trouble was when Shannon started attending a youth group where she met some peers who were involved with dark things. Of course, I didn't know that until much later. After meeting these kids, she began to dress in all black and lost a lot of weight, and her personality really began to change. This evolved over the course of the year into depression, cutting, half-hearted suicide attempts, and complete withdrawal from the family. Any interactions we did have resulted in Shannon yelling, screaming, and name-calling. It was the lowest point of my life for sure.

Through this time, I was in constant prayer asking God to break the chains of darkness that were imprisoning my daughter. This wasn't something I could have talked about to anyone except my husband and one or two friends, so it was a very lonely time. However, feeling so alone made me reach out to God in a way that I had never done before. I had always been a Christian, but I'd never been tested to the point that I had to totally trust Him. Now I needed to trust Him with my daughter's life.

During this time of prayer, God revealed to me several actions that my husband and I needed to take. Thus began the tough but unrelenting love approach with Shannon. The first thing God told me to do was to find all her CDs and throw them out. I decided to listen to a few before I did and was appalled at what I heard. Songs about killing others and yourself, profane and disgusting lyrics about women, sex, etc. I threw them all out and took away the CD player and radio. It was like God telling me to purge our house of the evil influences Shannon had brought into our home. Probably like most parents, I was unaware of what my children were listening to and watching on television.

Second, He told me to go through Shannon's room and read everything I could find and look for objects that represented evil. I found pentagrams, witchcraft books, and poems that Shannon had written about vampires, cutting, and death. I was shaken to the core after finding all of this, but it made me understand how deep into the darkness Shannon really was.

When you find your child in these circumstances, you have a choice to make. I hear the debate on talk shows all the time about whether you should respect your child's privacy and therefore not snoop around in their room. My opinion is that when you trust your child and things are going well, it is good to respect their privacy. But when you have suspicions or red flags about what is going on in your child's life, I strongly believe that you must use every possible way to find out the truth. Your child's life may depend on it. Shannon's did!

Also, when facing the truth about what your child is into, you need to decide if you are going to be the parent who loves her child enough to exhibit tough, caring love or you are going to try to be your child's friend. My experience with Shannon reinforced that she needed parents who would be firm and unwavering in our efforts to bring her back around. Believe me, this wasn't easy. However, with God's help we were able to do it. I've talked to so many parents in this situation and more often than not I've seen they were not able to step up and take the approach of tough, caring love. The parents who have sought my advice over the years and have been able to assume this approach have been much more successful in helping their child get through this very difficult time. Other parents either were so angry at their child that they couldn't inject the "love" into "tough love," or they just tried to be their child's friend through it all. As you heard from Shannon's perspective, the fact that we were able to hold true to a firm, but loving approach helped her end up where she is today.

If you have a spouse, make sure you talk about your roles in dealing with your child. There needs to be a "good cop, bad cop" approach. In our relationship, my husband was the firm hand, and although I was also firm, I tried to engage with Shannon on different levels. She was very uncommunicative during this time, so I would look for ways to get her to talk. It turned out that driving in the car was the only time she would open up, so we would drive around endlessly on some days and nights just so that I could get a sense of what she was thinking. Find those opportunities with your child. It may mean lying on the floor of their room talking to them, driving, or even engaging in physical sports. Just keep trying to find an environment that is non-threatening and conducive to allowing you to get an idea of where your child is.

Although the times I had with Shannon in the car were mostly calm and reasonable, there were times when she would have huge emotional outbursts and tell me she hated me. Those were devastating words to hear, but I refused to give up on her. I would grab her shoulders and look at her and say, "I know this isn't my child talking. I love you and I'll never give up hope for you—never!" Even though she would turn away from me and leave after these encounters, today Shannon says that my words and emotion still got through to her.

Shannon was fifteen years old at the time and was living in our house, so we had more control over her environment than someone whose child lives outside the house—but the same principles apply when dealing with a child who lives apart from you. An absolute key to Shannon's turnaround was disconnecting her from her peers who were so deeply involved in all the bad things that she needed to break free from.

We took her out of school and my husband homeschooled her. We put her on "house arrest" for a time. We took away her cell phone, and I even went to a spy store and picked up a device that monitored her calls. We took the TV out of her room and took her bedroom door off the hinges so we could observe her.

As you can imagine, she rebelled vehemently against all this, but we stuck to our guns. She was only allowed to go out of the house with us. We allowed her to go to our church's youth group, but we sat out front on the steps to make sure she didn't run away.

During this time, Shannon was suffering from severe depression, and along with cutting she made a half-hearted attempt at suicide by ingesting ibuprofen. She was hospitalized in a behavioral health center. While in the hospital, she met other teens who shared some of her issues, and they shared things they were doing, which gave Shannon more ideas, such as cutting. I first learned of this one day when I walked in on her while she was in the bathtub. I saw the scabs on her arm that outlined the word vampire. I thought I was going to faint on the spot as it was so incredibly distressing to me. What could be worse than a Christian family having a young daughter carve on her arm something that is related to a creature with a negative connotation?

I was overwhelmed with grief, but the grief made me pray and seek God even more.

Shannon did continue her cutting behavior for quite some time, and I came to understand that cutting wasn't really a suicide attempt but a way of releasing emotional pain. Cutting was her way of showing us the deep turmoil that was going on inside her. Cutting isn't talked about very much, but I believe it is common and one of the reasons Shannon wrote this book. This subject is still associated with a terrible stigma, so there is not much written about it. I couldn't find any books on the subject when I was researching how to help Shannon. If your child is engaging in this type of behavior, my advice is not to freak out but instead just get them the help that they need.

At the time, we were meeting with various counselors who were not much help. No one could get to the root of her depression and Goth-type behavior. Of course, Marshall and I had no idea at this time that she had gotten so deeply into witchcraft, and I didn't find out until a couple of years ago that Shannon had been raped.

We took Shannon home and got back into the "house-arrest" mode. Because Shannon was so depressed, I slept with her every night to make sure she didn't harm herself. Even though I'd get mad at her for her behavior and attitude, I just kept telling her, "I'm not going to give up on you." I prayed for her every waking moment that I could and cried out to God to please heal Shannon and reunite us as a family.

Although I wanted with all my heart to believe this would happen, I was beginning to wrestle with the fact that we might lose Shannon. I spent many days and nights sitting in my closet crying and praying (our house was so chaotic that it was the only place I could find some solitude).

Even though my husband and I were coping with this situation very differently, we did work hard to support each other during this time. His quiet hugs meant so much to me. If you are a couple going through this, know that it will test your marriage to the breaking point if you don't figure out a joint game plan on how to handle your child and how to support each other. Satan would like nothing better than to break up your marriage during this time of attack on your family.

Seeking professional help is critical when your child is withdrawn, depressed, or cutting. Shannon saw a psychiatrist regularly and was on high doses of antidepressants. We were referred to several counselors but most of them had a secular view, which was, "It's a stage. She will grow out of it. Give her some room and don't be too strict." I knew through my prayer time and verses that God gave me, such as Proverbs 3:5-7, that this counsel was the opposite of what God was leading us to do, so we didn't continue counseling as a family.

Having said this, I know counselors can be very helpful in situations with rebellious and depressed teenagers. Just make sure you find someone who shares your perspective about how to help your child. No one knows your child better than you do. You must assume the advocacy role for your child during these situations.

If you are a Christian, I would really suggest seeking out a Christian counselor who is experienced but young enough to relate to your child. Shannon had a great Christian counselor who ended up helping her and who communicated well with us. We will be eternally grateful for her help. It was this counselor who went with Shannon, my husband, and me to see a pastor at our church who specialized in helping troubled kids, especially those who had been involved in cult-like activities. He talked straight to Shannon and told her and us that the chance of coming out of this dark side was about 10 percent in his experience—unless Shannon was willing to acknowledge to God all she had been involved in and ask for forgiveness.

After I heard this, I remember having an out-of-body experience during the rest of our meeting because the odds he was giving us were so low. Shannon did pray with him, but I think it was more out of fear than anything else. When we got home, I remember asking her if I could pray with her asking God to intervene in her life and she said yes. Things began to get a little better after that, but she was still wearing black all the time and was depressed—but not as angry and rebellious as before.

A few months later we were in an evening service at our church. Shannon didn't want to sit next to us, so she sat at the end of a pew with a girl she had met. In all honesty, I was surprised this girl had reached out to her because Shannon was pretty scary looking in all her Goth dress and accessories. I remain thankful to her for loving Shannon when it wasn't easy to love Shannon.

At the end of the service, the pastor had us pray, and he offered an invitation for people to come up front and give their lives to Christ, which supposedly Shannon had done in third grade. When we opened our eyes after the prayer, I looked over at Shannon and she was gone! I started to cry because I thought she had run away as she had done before when we were in church. I turned to my husband and told him we needed to find her. As we were getting up, someone came up to us and asked if we were looking for Shannon and said she had come forward at the pastor's invitation to accept Christ as her Lord and Savior. I began to sob uncontrollably. I was so thankful to God for this miracle. This was the turning point and the start of her healing process.

As the months progressed, Shannon's attitude began to change, her depression started lifting, and we talked about how she could regain our trust. She had hurt our family deeply, including her younger sister, and we told her she would have to prove to us over time that we could trust her. Until then there would continue to be many restrictions on who she could see and talk to, and she wasn't allowed to go anywhere by herself, except to the house of one Christian friend.

A few months later she handed me all her black clothes and said she didn't need them anymore. That was one happy day! Shannon then began attending a Christian high school and became a cheerleader, which helped her once again become the child we knew. It was about this time that she felt God's strong calling to pursue a degree in mental health counseling. She never wavered from this, and now has achieved that goal and will be helping others who are going through the things she experienced. She is a wonderful counselor now because of everything she had to go through.

Here are some of the lessons I learned as a parent through Shannon's journey:

- Never give up hope!

- Advocate for your child. You know them best.

- Trust God and engage in intercessory prayer for your child. If your child is living in your house, you still have spiritual authority over them.

- Be the parent they need, not the friend they want.

- Control the environment and limit external influences.

- Seek out young, experienced Christian counselors who can relate to your child.

- Forgive yourself for the mistakes you make.

- If you are married, work out the game plan with your spouse and support each other through this.

- Don't neglect other members of the family. Unfortunately, our younger daughter felt neglected during this time because we were so wrapped up in trying to save Shannon's life. She has struggled with some of the memories of that time and only recently has begun her healing process. In hindsight we really should have been more available and supportive to her during this time as well. We didn't realize that she was feeling so vulnerable at that time, but this reinforces the fact that situations like this impact the entire family in different ways.

- Don't let your anger toward your child cause you to become bitter and unapproachable. Remember your child needs you more than ever during this time. If you become angry and bitter, the chances of your child turning his or her life around become less. You are the lifeline, whether your child deserves it or not.

I understand the pain and emotional roller coaster that a prodigal child brings. Having gone through this, I truly know what it means to have your heart broken. However, don't give up hope, no matter what. As you have read in Shannon's story, it is possible through tough, caring love and prayer to break the chains that hold your child from the life God intended them to have. Remember, nothing is impossible with God. I look at Shannon now and marvel at how God took a very dark time in her life and turned it into a beacon of light for others. I am immensely proud of her for having the courage to write this book. She is an inspiration to me!

—Sherrie Sitarik

SHOWING YOUR SUPPORT: TOP 10 THINGS TO REMEMBER

1. Listen: Be an active listener; be genuine and supportive in your statements. An example of this would be: "So what I heard you say is..."

2. Watch: Keep an eye on behavior and attitude changes.

3. Be supportive: Show empathy and understanding when your teen talks to you.

4. Do not judge: Try not to use blaming statements such as "You _____." Instead, use statements such as, "I feel _____."

5. Pray: You have spiritual authority over your teen. Pray for them and for your guidance.

6. Seek professional help: Know your options when in a crisis and engage your teen in the decision-making process when possible.

7. Do not be afraid to act: You have authority over your teen. Try to be a parent more than a friend to them.

8. Set boundaries: Teens need structure as well as independence. Set rules and consequences in the home.

9. Choose your battles: Choose what is important to you. Think before you act. A good question to remember is, "Will this hurt my teen or my family in any way?" If the answer is no then let that battle go.

10. Do not give up: This is the most important. Never give up on your teen. Show them you are with them for the entire journey.

I'll say it again: don't give up! This is the single most important advice I can give to you. My mother never gave up on me, and to this day I appreciate it more than any other thing she has done for me. Your loved one who is hurting may push you away and say some of the most hurtful words to you that you could imagine but stay by their side. Show them you love them and will never leave them during this tough time. Don't push things on them that they do not want to hear. Instead give it up to God and trust He will take care of each worry you have today. Be their cheerleader. You won't regret it in the end.

National

- **National Suicide Prevention Lifeline:** 1-800-273-8255

- **National Suicide Hotline:** 1-800-Suicide (800-784-2433)

- **Parent Hotline:** 1-800-840-6537

- **National Drug Information Treatment and Referral Hotline:** 1-800-662-Help (4357)

- **National Domestic Violence Hotline:** 1-800-799-SAFE (7233)

- **National Rape Crisis Hotline:** 1-800-656-4673

- **National Sexual Assault Hotline:** 1-800-656-HOPE (4673)

- **Self-Injury S.A.F.E:** 1-800-DONT-CUT (800-366-8288)

- **Teen Hope Line:** 1-800-394-HOPE (4673)

Central Florida

- **Orlando Crisis/Suicide Hotline:** 407-425-2624

- **Central Florida Center for Drug-Free Living:** 407-245-0014

- **Aspire Health:** 407-875-3700

- **The Healing Tree Sexual Trauma Recovery Center:** 407-317-7430

- **House of Hope:** 407-843-8686

- **Orlando Teen Crisis Line:** 407-841-7413

- **University Behavioral Center:** 407-281-7000

- **Central Florida Behavioral Hospital:** 407-370-0111

- **Perfectly Imperfect Counseling:** 407-392-9398

SHARE WITH OTHERS

I hope you enjoyed reading *A Purpose for the Pain* and you were able to find inspiration and encouragement as you read through the different chapters.

If you believe this book has the potential to encourage others, here are some things I'd like to ask you to consider...

- Share a positive post about the book on Facebook, Instagram, or other social media, and use #APurposeForThePain.

- I would also love to connect with you on a more personal level. Please feel free to send me an email at info@perfectlyimperfectcounseling.com

- Consider ordering a copy of my follow-up book, *Dance it Out, Girl: Navigating the Mess and Beauty of Motherhood.*

- Order extra copies of this book to share with others. To order copies of any of my books or to learn more about the counseling services I offer, please visit my website at:
www.perfectlyimperfectcounseling.com

Let your journey in healing begin today!

Uncover your true potential. Become who you are meant to be. You are not alone. Life is your journey. Find your passion. Solve everyday issues. Develop more meaningful relationships. Let go of stress and enjoy life more. Healing is your power.

Be empowered! Gain the support you deserve in a safe environment. You can obtain positive growth, healing, and well-being through your counseling experience.

Post-Traumatic Stress Disorder

Self-Injury

Couples Counseling

Family Counseling

Parenting Support

Stress Management

Perfectly Imperfect
Counseling

www.perfectlyimperfectcounseling.com

ALSO AVAILABLE

DANCE IT OUT GIRL!

Navigating the Mess and Beauty of Motherhood

This book is a wonderful resource and guide for all mothers tying to navigate through the beauty and mess of motherhood. Each chapter is filled with relatable stories, encouragement and professional advise on how to cope during those hard moments of motherhood.

www.perfectlyimperfectcounseling.com/resources

CPSIA information can be obtained
at www.ICGtesting.com
Printed in the USA
BVHW042144141221
624087BV00014B/890